Crafts

**through the year
for 4-7 year olds**

Maureen Davies

Michael O'Mara Books Limited

For Anne with love

First published in 1990 by
Michael O'Mara Books Limited, 9 Lion Yard,
11–13 Tremadoc Road, London SW4 7NF

Copyright © 1990 by Maureen Davies

All rights reserved.
No part of this publication
may be reproduced, stored in a
retrieval system or transmitted, in
any form or by any means without the
prior permission in writing of the publisher, nor
be otherwise circulated in any form of binding
or cover other than that in which it is
published and without a similar
condition being imposed on
the subsequent purchaser.

A CIP catalogue record for this book
is available from the British Library

ISBN 1-85479-007-2 (hardback)
ISBN 1-85479-012-9 (paperback)

Design by: Richard Souper
Illustrations by: Wladec Szechter

Typeset by Florencetype Ltd, Kewstoke, Avon
Printed and bound by Cox and Wyman Ltd,
Reading

CONTENTS

Introduction 4

A List of Essential Craft Materials 5

SPRING

Pasta/Pulse Pictures	7
Valentine Card	8
Wax Resist Picture	9
Favourite Dinners	10
Painted Eggs	11
Easter Bunny Picture	12
Easter Crowns	13
Clay Houses	14
Group Activity – A Village	16

SUMMER

Butterflies	18
Fish Mosaic	20
Fan Bird	22
Stone Painting/Sculpture	24
Clay Butterflies	25
Fabric Collage House	26
A Group Picture – Bees	28
Group Activity – Dinosaur Land and Clay Dinosaurs	30
Shoe Box House	32

AUTUMN

Clay Pots	33
Fruit and Vegetable Printing	34
Hedgehogs and Squirrels	36
Cat Masks	38
Leaf Spatter Pictures	39
Walking Witch	40
Fruit and Vegetable People	42
Group Activity – Autumn Tree	44
Cardboard Fireworks	47

WINTER

Folded Paper Snowmen	48
Window Christmas Card	50
Angel Mobile	52
Clown Finger Puppets	53
The Three Bears	54
Biscuit Tins	56
Biscuits to Fill the Tins	58
Wallpaper Trees	60
Group Activity – Play Dough Pictures	62

INTRODUCTION

This book is intended to provide a simple step-by-step guide to art and craft activities through the year. Aimed particularly at inspiring the non-artistic parent, it provides an appropriate seasonal craft idea for almost every week with straightforward and – I hope – foolproof instructions. A number of ideas included are suitable for group activity – perhaps when your children have friends over for the day, for example.

No particular skill is needed on the part of the parent or minder, other than an ability to make fairly accurate copies of the diagrams in the book. If you're not sure of your ability to copy the diagrams, make a rough template on squared paper first. It's a good idea in any case to make templates on card, so that you can keep them to use again and again – hedgehogs and squirrels, for instance, are always popular with small children.

'Adult Preparation' is obviously aimed at you, the parent or minder. 'Making Up' is for the children to do – though they'll still need a bit of help from time to time, especially if sharp scissors are called for.

All the activities in this book have been tried and tested by the pupils of Sandle Manor School, Hampshire.

A LIST OF ESSENTIAL CRAFT MATERIALS

Round-ended scissors – one pair per child saves arguments

Pencils

Rubbers

Felt-tipped pens – the non-toxic kind and for safety's sake check they have a hole in the top

Chunky good quality wax crayons

Pastels – oil and chalk

Paints – WASHABLE! Ready-mixed poster colours are the easiest to use. Add a few drops of washing-up liquid to make them easier to clean off

Paint brushes – chunky short-handled ones are easier for small children to use

Glue – use sticks wherever possible, they make much less mess. When a thicker layer is needed, use white PVA glue which is washable and dries clear

Glue spreaders – if you don't have a plastic one, use strips of card. Although these don't last for long, at least they don't need washing

Containers for paint and glue – again, use disposable ones such as yoghurt pots

Clay – 'New Clay' is self-hardening and does away with the need to fire

Plasticine – if this is too hard, put it in a warm place for a couple of hours to make it more pliable

Card – white and coloured

Paper – ALL SORTS: tissue, gummed, sugar, and plenty of plain white paper

Newspaper – always ensure that surfaces are well covered with a thick layer, EXCEPT when working with clay (which will stick to the paper)

Painting overall – a plastic one with sleeves large enough to fit easily over clothes is ideal for messy work. A good alternative is to cut down an old shirt

Glitter and sequins – anything sparkly is fun but needs to be applied with great care over trays or a sheet of paper

Tools for clay, plasticine and play dough are easily found in the home – palette knives, pencils, rolling pins, biscuit cutters, etc

OTHER USEFUL ITEMS FROM AROUND THE HOME INCLUDE:

Paper plates (plastic or polystyrene ones can snap – and paint doesn't adhere to them easily)

Cardboard tubes

Magazines (the cheaper colour ones are best for tearing into pieces)

Fabric and wool scraps

Drinking straws

Doilies

Pasta, pulses and seeds

Wallpaper scraps

Shoe boxes

Paper clips

Cotton wool

Corks and cotton reels

A selection of smooth pebbles from a beach

PASTA/PULSE PICTURES

MATERIALS
1. Sugar paper or thin card for a stronger picture
2. Glue and spreaders
3. Pencils
4. An assortment of lentils, peas, pasta shapes in a variety of colours, put out in separate small pots and containers

ADULT PREPARATION
1. With younger children, draw a simple outline for them to fill in
2. To extend the colour range, dye rice and pasta in a solution of water and food colouring

MAKING UP
1. Draw a simple picture outline
2. Work on the collage a small area at a time. Cover with glue and fix the pasta or pulses on. Try not to get them mixed up in their containers. Think about using a particular colour or texture for one area, a contrasting one next to it

SUBJECT IDEAS
Animals, dinosaurs, houses, flowers, butterflies, birds, or simply patterns of different shapes

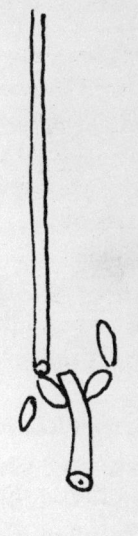

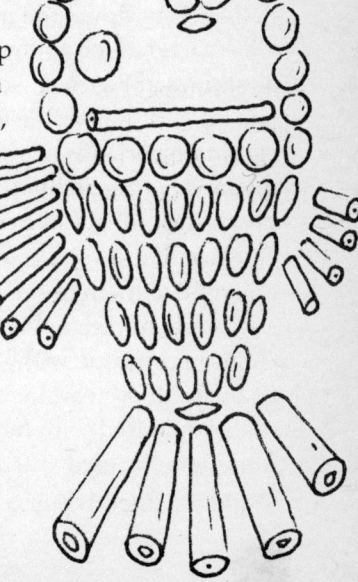

VALENTINE CARD

MATERIALS
1. Sheet of card (suggested size 318mm × 254mm) in a pale colour
2. Piece of red paper, either plain or gummed, about 18cm × 16cm
3. Scissors
4. Pencils
5. Glue stick
6. Felt-tipped pens
7. Paper doilies

ADULT PREPARATION
1. Fold each end of the card to meet in the middle as shown in Figure 1
2. Draw a heart as large as possible on to the red paper (try to keep the two sides even)

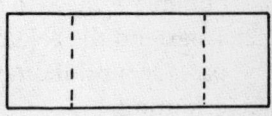

Fig. 1

MAKING UP
1. Cut out the outlined heart, then fold it in half and cut down the middle
2. Glue each half on to the front of the card as shown in Figure 2, so that the heart joins down the middle when the card is closed (experience has shown that a lot of guidance is needed here – children in a hurry stick hearts all over the place!)
3. Cut lace-like strips about 1cm wide from a doily. Glue them to the edge of the heart – a couple of pieces will be all younger children can cope with
4. Draw another heart inside the card which can be coloured with felt tips
5. Complete the card with an appropriate message

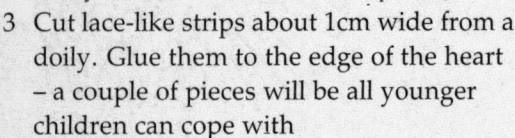

Fig. 2

WAX RESIST PICTURE

MATERIALS
1. Wax crayons or oil pastels
2. Very thin paint in a dark colour
3. Large brushes or a spray (see leaf spatter pictures, page 39)
4. White paper

ADULT PREPARATION
Mix up some very watery poster paint in black or very dark blue. The consistency should be such that it does not adhere to the wax crayon when applied over the top. It is a good idea to check this before beginning

PAINTING
1. Draw a colourful picture using pastels or crayons. This should contain some solid areas of bright colour, as well as some empty spaces, for the best results. Encourage the children to press quite hard
2. Paint over the entire picture. The paint should only adhere to the paper showing between the drawing
3. If preferred, spray the picture with paint, to give a more speckled background

FURTHER IDEAS
This technique is particularly suited to showing off brightly coloured subjects such as flowers, birds, and butterflies. It is also effective for night scenes, such as fireworks

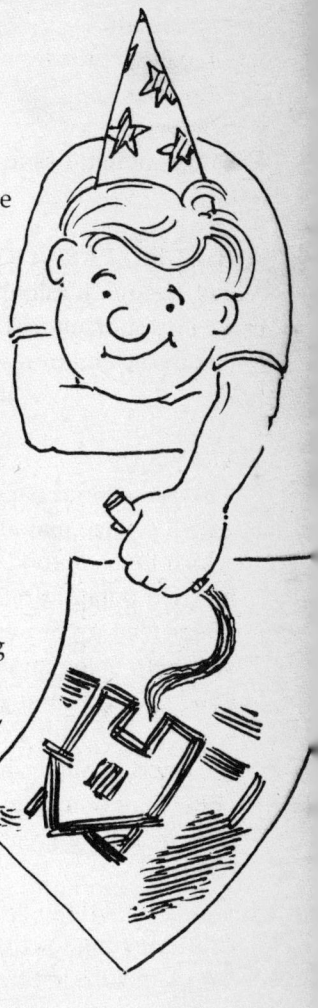

FAVOURITE DINNERS

Don't attempt this with more than two children at a time, as a lot of help is needed with the ideas and the cutting out.

MATERIALS
1. Paper plate
2. Glue and spreader
3. Glue stick
4. Scissors
5. Scraps of felt, tissue, cotton wool, pasta, etc

ADULT PREPARATION
None! Though it might be a good idea to make one yourself first as a guide. Take time to talk to the children about their favourite food

MAKING UP
1. Cut out felt and paper, taking time to see which collage materials best represent which items of food. Use cotton wool for mashed potato, dried pasta and tiny bits of screwed-up brown and red tissue for spaghetti bolognaise. Brown felt makes good sausages and eggs can be cut out of white paper with a yellow circle drawn in the middle. Make chips by cutting out oblongs of orange gummed paper and peas by rolling green bits of tissue into balls
2. Stick all the food on to the plate with glue
3. As a finishing touch, decorate the edge of the plate with felt tips

PAINTED EGGS

MATERIALS
1. Hard-boiled eggs
2. Felt-tipped pens
3. Varnish
4. Odd scraps of wool, fabric and ribbon
5. Small pieces of white or pink card
6. Glue sticks
7. Egg cups (glue stick caps also make good stands)

ADULT PREPARATION
1. Hard boil at least one egg per child
2. Cut out arms and legs from the card, copying the diagrams
3. Cut out any clothes required (e.g. soldier's hat, Humpty Dumpty's bow tie) from scraps of felt, fabric or paper

MAKING UP
1. Give each child an egg on which a face should be drawn with felt tips
2. Turn the eggs into characters by adding hair (use wool, or colour with felt tips) and clothes (cut out from scraps and stick on, or colour on)
3. Colour arms and legs, adding hands, gloves, socks, shoes, boots, etc
4. Stick the arms to the back of the egg near the base and fold forward as shown. Glue the legs to the base of the egg
5. Varnish the eggs if desired and place in stands

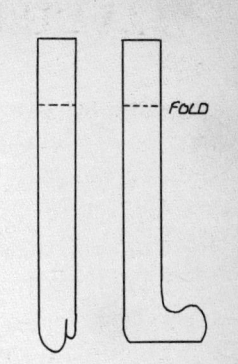

EASTER BUNNY PICTURE

MATERIALS
1 Card for templates
2 Pencils
3 Scissors
4 Gummed paper
5 Cotton wool
6 Felt-tipped pens
7 Coloured paper for background, about 30cm × 23cm

ADULT PREPARATION
Make templates, copying the drawing below

MAKING UP
1 Draw round the templates and cut out of gummed paper a body, a head and two ears
2 Stick the pieces on to the coloured paper. Keep a close eye on the positioning while this is going on
3 Stick a small cotton-wool ball at the base of the body to form a tail. (This picture is a back view, but a lot of children will still want to draw a face!)
4 Draw grass and flowers round the rabbit
5 Draw whiskers from each side of the head in black felt tip. This is probably best done by an adult

NOTE: You could also make a similar Easter Bunny using fabric scraps.

EASTER CROWNS

MATERIALS
1. A strip of card about 10cm deep and long enough to fit round a child's head. Use either white or coloured card
2. Thin card for making chicks and flowers
3. Scissors
4. Felt-tipped pens, crayons or gummed paper

ADULT PREPARATION
Copy the drawings opposite on to the thin card to make some chicks and flowers

MAKING UP
1. Decorate the strip of card to form the base for the crown. Either colour patterns in felt tips, or cut out and stick on shapes of coloured paper
2. Cut out the flowers and chicks and simply paint or colour with felt tips. If preferred, stalks of green card can be stapled on afterwards. The chick could be made from cotton wool dyed yellow in food colouring with a black bead eye, or dot with a black marker

TO COMPLETE
1. Fold the decorated strip to fit the child's head and staple the ends together
2. Staple chicks and flowers to the crown at intervals
3. You can make additional decorations with tissue paper streamers or ribbons stapled to each side and tied in a bow under the chin

CLAY HOUSES

MATERIALS
1. A lump of clay (the self-hardening kind is best) about the size of a tennis ball
2. Rolling pin
3. Knife
4. An assortment of clay tools – anything that will 'dig out' or make marks in the clay, such as nails, ends of pencils, lolly sticks; old cotton reels or lids pushed in to make circles or small building bricks to make squares; old combs

ADULT PREPARATION
1. Cover the work surface with oil cloth
2. Be prepared to give plenty of help all the way through

MAKING
1. Divide the clay into two pieces
2. Shape the first into a rectangular block for the basic house front. Roll the second piece into a rectangle and position it to form the roof
3. Discuss how to add details and how to simulate the various materials used to build houses. Doors and windows can be made either by rolling out pieces of clay and cutting into shape, or by pressing suitably shaped objects into the clay. Thatch can be suggested by making scratch marks with a pointed object, while tiles could be made by taking tiny balls of clay and pressing them flat on the roof in

rows. Chimneys could be added and creeper scratched on the wall

TO COMPLETE
The houses are probably too heavy to fire and so are best left to harden in their natural state without being painted.

GROUP ACTIVITY – A VILLAGE

MATERIALS
1. Clay houses (see previous page)
2. Two large sheets of background paper, one green
3. Paints: grey for a road, blue for sky, green for hills and trees. Put the last two in wide-necked containers for sponge-painting
4. Pieces of sponge that a child can comfortably hold for painting
5. A collection of small twigs to represent tree trunks
6. Oddments of sponge for the leaves and bushes (offcuts about 1cm thick are ideal)
7. Small lumps of plasticine to make bases for the trees
8. Scissors
9. Paint brushes

ADULT PREPARATION
1. On the green paper draw in some roads and a river
2. On the second sheet draw the outline of some hills
3. Mix up the paints
4. If there's enough room, it's a good idea to set up one table for painting and another for tree-making

PAINTING
1. Organize a group to paint the road (grey) and river (blue) and sponge-paint the hills and sky. A better effect is achieved if the colours aren't completely solid, but rather

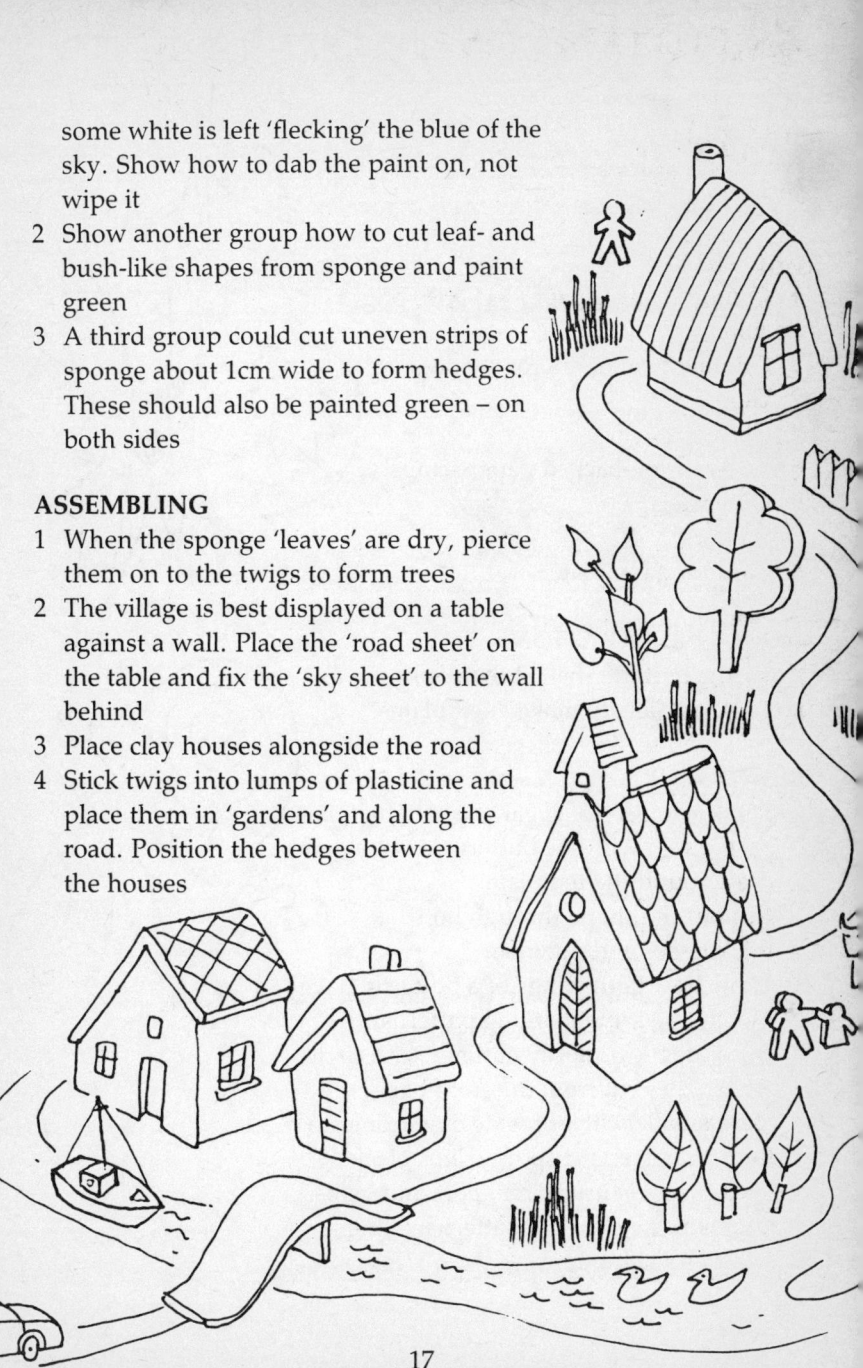

some white is left 'flecking' the blue of the sky. Show how to dab the paint on, not wipe it
2 Show another group how to cut leaf- and bush-like shapes from sponge and paint green
3 A third group could cut uneven strips of sponge about 1cm wide to form hedges. These should also be painted green – on both sides

ASSEMBLING
1 When the sponge 'leaves' are dry, pierce them on to the twigs to form trees
2 The village is best displayed on a table against a wall. Place the 'road sheet' on the table and fix the 'sky sheet' to the wall behind
3 Place clay houses alongside the road
4 Stick twigs into lumps of plasticine and place them in 'gardens' and along the road. Position the hedges between the houses

🦋 BUTTERFLIES

It's a good idea to find some pictures of butterflies to look at before you start this project.

MATERIALS
1. Coloured sugar paper – choose bright colours
2. Gummed paper and/or shapes
3. Glue
4. Glitter
5. Shiny or foil-backed paper scraps
6. Oil pastels
7. Scissors
8. Card for a template

ADULT PREPARATION
Copy the butterfly half shown opposite as large as possible to make a template

MAKING UP
1. Fold each piece of sugar paper in half, line up the fold with the butterfly's body and draw round the template
2. Cut out the shape through both thicknesses and open out
3. Show how both wings of a butterfly have exactly the same marking patterns
4. Decorate the butterfly outlines with circles and shapes cut from different papers. Place smaller circles inside larger ones to form characteristic spots. Thick black marker pen is useful for spots and veins. Use oil pastels for the patterns. Glitter adds a finishing touch

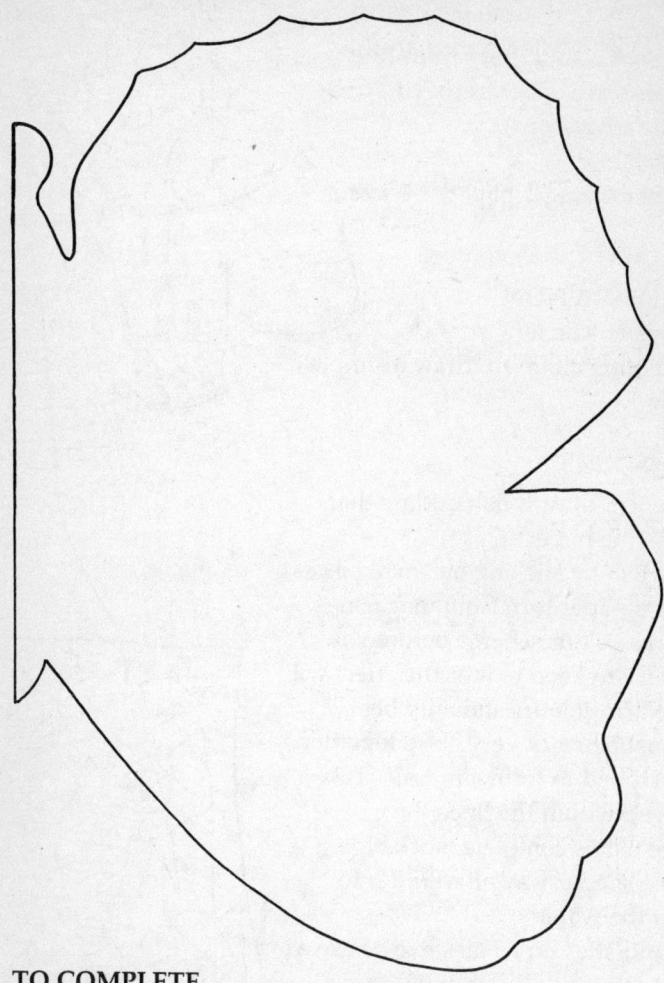

TO COMPLETE
1 Arrange several butterflies haphazardly on a large sheet of blue paper. Make or paint flowers along the bottom
2 Decorate both sides of the butterfly wings and hang up as a mobile

FISH MOSAIC

MATERIALS
1 A selection of colour magazines (the cheaper ones are better as they have a softer edge when torn)
2 Glue stick
3 White paper or sugar paper, A4 size
4 Pencil

ADULT PREPARATION
1 Cut the paper to size
2 For very young children, draw a simple fish shape

MAKING UP
1 With a pencil, draw a fish outline that nearly fills the paper
2 Fill in the fish by sticking on small pieces of coloured paper torn from magazines. Decide on a colour scheme before you start and try to keep to it or the effect will be lost. Warm colours show up best. Pieces must be stuck very close together and overlapped to form a mosaic. Take care to keep within the lines
3 When the fish is complete, stick blue pieces in a similar way all round it to represent the water
4 Cut out and stick on a black eye or use a button

FURTHER IDEAS
There are many pictures that can be made using this technique, and here are just a few ideas. Remember always to have a strong

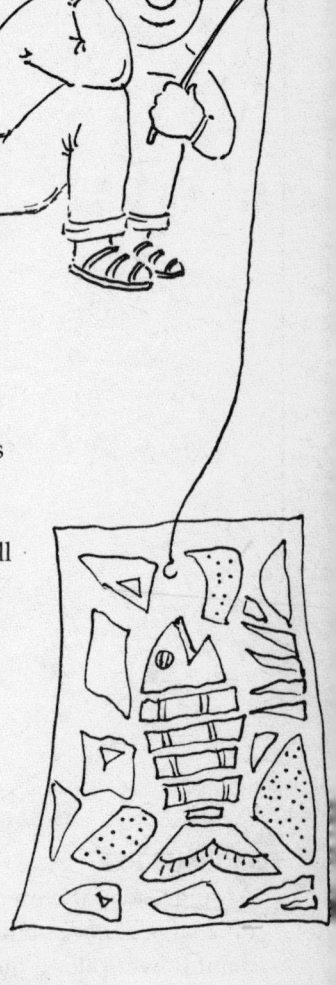

contrast in colour between subject and background:
a) House against a blue sky
b) Flowers on green grass
c) Geometric shapes on a contrasting colour
d) A bright butterfly on a dark background

FAN BIRD

MATERIALS
1. Thin card – A4 size – in white or a pale colour
2. A4 sheet of white or coloured paper for wings
3. Felt-tipped pens or crayons
4. Scissors
5. Coloured tissue paper

ADULT PREPARATION
1. Copy out the bird opposite on to the card
2. Cut out strips of tissue about 3cm wide to make tail streamers

MAKING UP
1. Cut out the bird from the card
2. Colour in – using lots of patterns and bright colours. Both sides must be coloured, which can get rather tedious for younger children in one session
3. Colour in white paper for wings
4. Fold over about 3cm along one long edge of the paper and then fold it back on itself, like a concertina. Continue across the whole sheet

TO COMPLETE
1. An adult should make a slit in the side of the bird long enough to slide through the folded wing. When in position the wings should fan out on each side
2. Staple tissue paper streamers to the tail
3. These birds are most effective hanging from the ceiling

FURTHER IDEAS
The birds can be decorated in many ways.
For instance:
a) Gummed paper cut into feather shapes or shiny foil paper
b) Tissue paper screwed into balls and stuck on
c) With wax crayons or oil pastels
d) Blotting paper wings can have spots of watery paint or food colouring dropped on to them

STONE PAINTING/ SCULPTURE

MATERIALS
1. A selection of smooth pebbles
2. Paint and/or felt-tipped pens
3. Clear polyurethane varnish
4. Plasticine
5. Glue

ADULT PREPARATION
Ensure that the stones are clean and dry

WORKING
1. Spread the pebbles out on a table and let children make their own choice
2. Encourage children to look hard at their stones and to use their imaginations. Some are easier than others – a triangular stone in two colours might suggest the beak of a bird; an even round shape, a ladybird. Other stones can simply be decorated with bright patterns, but take the time to cover them really thickly with colour, particularly where felt tips are being used
3. Sometimes plasticine can hold several small stones together to create little animals, though usually a very strong glue is needed
4. Varnish the stones carefully – allow one side to dry before varnishing the other
5. The finished stones can simply be displayed on a sheet of coloured paper, or they can be turned into paperweights by gluing a small piece of green baize to the base

🦋 CLAY BUTTERFLIES

MATERIALS
1. Clay – the self-hardening variety
2. Paints in bright colours
3. Clear polyurethane varnish
4. Rolling pin
5. Knife
6. Stiff card to make a template

ADULT PREPARATION
Copy the drawing of a butterfly on to stiff card and cut out

MAKING UP
1. Give each child a lump of clay about the size of a tennis ball
2. Roll this out evenly to a thickness about 1cm
3. Hold the template firmly on top of the clay while the shape is cut out with a knife (considerable help will be needed here to keep the different elements in place)
4. When the butterflies have hardened (or been kiln-fired if the clay is not self-hardening), decorate them with paints. Take care to ensure that both wings are the same

TO COMPLETE
1. Varnish the painted butterflies
2. When dry, mount them on dark coloured card
3. As a final touch make two holes in the top and thread through a ribbon loop to hang the pictures

NOTE: Older children might like to make butterfly pendants. Follow the same procedure, but make smaller butterflies and put a hole in the top of each wing. Thread through a ribbon or coloured string.

FABRIC COLLAGE HOUSE

Try to give the children as wide a variety as possible of colours, prints and textures, so that the finished results will be as individual as possible.

MATERIALS
1. Selection of cotton fabric remnants.
   Suggested types:
   - Needlecord for the roof
   - Checks/gingham for windows
   - Floral pattern for flower border
2. Pinking shears
3. Coloured paper
4. Glue – white PVA
5. Felt-tipped pens or gummed paper

ADULT PREPARATION
1. Copy the house shapes opposite on to paper, to the size you want. Use stiff paper or card if you think you'll want to keep them to use again
2. Use as patterns to draw round and cut the shapes out of material. Use pinking shears to give a neat, non-fraying edge

MAKING UP
1. Give each child a sheet of coloured paper on which to 'build' the house
2. Glue the pieces down using only a little glue. Be careful to position the pieces in a sensible order: walls, followed by the roof, then a floral strip along the base of the house. Finally stick on the door and windows

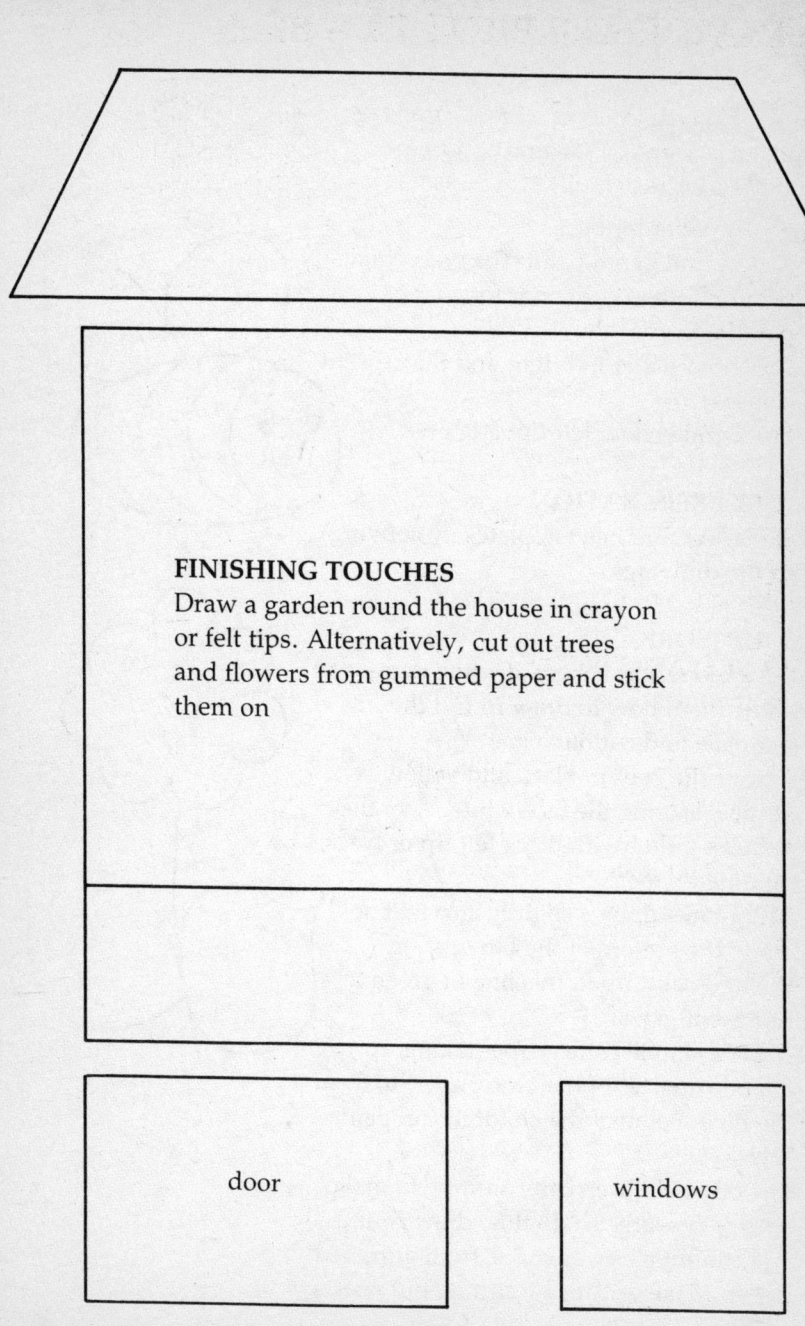

FINISHING TOUCHES
Draw a garden round the house in crayon or felt tips. Alternatively, cut out trees and flowers from gummed paper and stick them on

door

windows

A GROUP PICTURE – BEES

MATERIALS
1. Two large sheets of blue paper for background
2. White paper for bees
3. Yellow and green paint (the green in a wide-mouthed container for sponge-painting)
4. Gummed paper in bright and fluorescent colours
5. Black and yellow felt-tipped pens

ADULT PREPARATION
Make flower and bee templates by copying from the drawings

GROUP WORK
1. Give each child a sheet of white paper and show them how to draw round the template and cut out a bee
2. Colour the bees in black and yellow stripes, leaving the face white. Add the features either with black felt tip or black gummed paper
3. Meanwhile draw a slightly curved line along the bottom of the blue paper. Sponge-paint up to this line in green to represent grass
4. Draw a simple cone shape (taking up about a quarter of the blue paper) to form the hive. Some of the children can paint it yellow
5. The other children can continue to make bees or flowers. To do this, draw round and cut out a flower shape from gummed paper. Make centres by cutting out circles

from yellow and orange paper and sticking on; different shades are more effective. Finally make stalks and leaves from green paper using the diagram as a guide

TO COMPLETE
1 Make irregular brick-shaped lines in black over the yellow hive and block in a small rectangular shape at the bottom for a door
2 Arrange the flowers along the bottom of the picture (over the grass) and position the bees all over the background – some flying in, some flying out, others settling on flowers

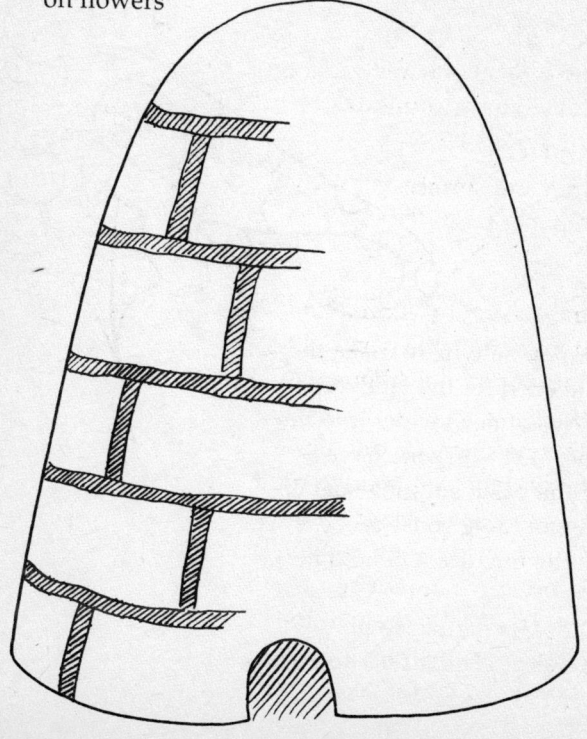

GROUP ACTIVITY – DINOSAUR LAND and CLAY DINOSAURS

Small children love dinosaurs, so this is sure to be popular – but it is also *very* messy!

MATERIALS
For the landscape
1. Lots of newspaper
2. Wallpaper paste
3. A large container for mixing in – an old baby's bath is ideal
4. An old tray or board
5. Paints and brushes
6. Bits of cardboard (egg boxes are especially good)
7. Glue or plasticine

For the dinosaurs
1. Self-hardening clay
2. Paints
3. Varnish

ADULT PREPARATION
1. Cover all children and surfaces!
2. Mix up the wallpaper paste

MAKING UP
The landscape
1. Children will enjoy helping to make the papier mâché needed for the landscape. First tear up strips of newspaper into the mixing container. Let everyone have a turn at stirring the paste and newspaper mixture until a moulding consistency is reached (when the mixture will hold its shape)
2. To form the landscape, crumple up cardboard boxes as a base for hills and use

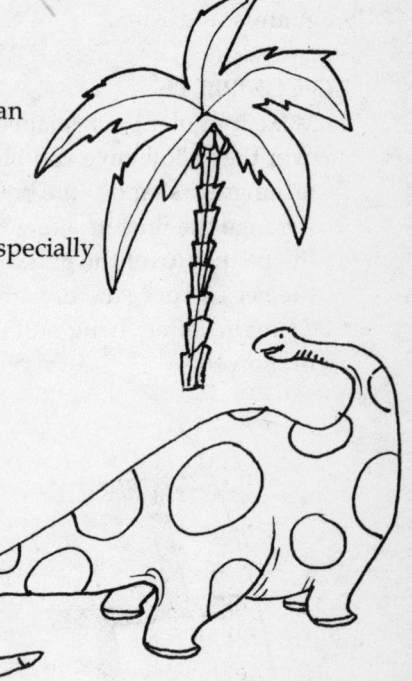

glue or plasticine to secure them to the baseboard
3 Cover the entire surface with papier mâché, moulding it over the boxes to look like a landscape. Turn one of the hills into a volcano by making a hole in the top and flames out of red foil paper stuck inside
4 The landscape will take several days to dry. After that, paint it in suitable colours

The dinosaurs
1 Look at pictures of dinosaurs (plastic models can also be helpful) and talk about the texture of the skin, different types of animal and their comparative sizes
2 Give each child a lump of clay about the size of a tennis ball; some will want to copy a picture, others will think up their own particular dinosaur. Scaly marks can be drawn into the clay and spines formed by squeezing the clay out. Be prepared to give plenty of help
3 When the dinosaurs are dry, paint them and varnish

TO COMPLETE
1 Position the clay models on the landscape
2 If there's space, position the board against a wall where a backdrop of painted sky and hills can be fixed to complete the picture

SHOE BOX HOUSE

MATERIALS
1. Shoe box
2. Paint and brushes
3. Glue and spreaders
4. Cotton reels or egg box for chimneys
5. Cardboard tubes for chimneys

ADULT PREPARATION
1. Turn out the rim of the lid to make it flat, cutting the corners
2. Bend the lid in half to form a roof shape
3. Turn the box upside-down and draw in doors and windows

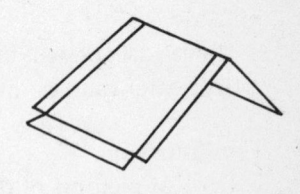

MAKING UP
1. Spread glue along the two short edges of the lid and stick on to the upturned box to form a roof
2. Cut out doors and windows (be prepared to help, especially if the card is very stiff)
3. Paint the house. Older children might be guided to think about building materials, and represent tiles and bricks
4. To make chimneys, make a tab by cutting two slits at the base of a card tube and folding gently outwards. Glue the underside of the tab and stick the tube on the top of the roof
5. Form chimney pots from cotton reels fitted inside the top of the tubes

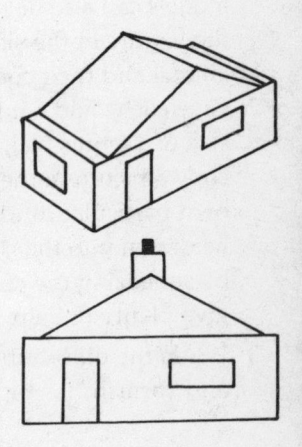

TO COMPLETE
If you make several houses, you can arrange them on a large sheet of green paper to make a street or village scene

🌿 CLAY POTS

MATERIALS
1. Self-hardening clay
2. Poster paints
3. Clear polyurethane varnish

ADULT PREPARATION
Break off a piece of clay for each child – about the size of a tennis ball

MAKING
1. Work the clay into a smooth ball – small children may find this quite hard work
2. Place the thumb firmly into the centre of this ball and keep enlarging the hole by squeezing between thumb and fingers, turning the pot as you go

NOTE: Children often make the hole far too large, so the sides of the pot become too thin and collapse!

3. When an approximate pot shape has been achieved, smooth over the surface with fingertips and leave to dry for 24 hours

TO COMPLETE
1. When they are dry, paint the pots with simple patterns such as dots and zigzags
2. A coat of clear varnish does much to enhance the finished pot and helps prevent the paint rubbing off on to hands and clothes!

FRUIT AND VEGETABLE PRINTING

MATERIALS
1. A selection of hard fruits and vegetables such as potato, carrot, parsnip, swede, apple, or celery
2. Thick paint in saucers or lids
3. Sugar paper
4. Sharp vegetable knife

ADULT PREPARATION
1. Cut up the fruit and vegetables in different ways. Remember the pieces should be a suitable size for holding and aim for as wide a variety of shapes as possible – potatoes can be halved or chipped, carrots cut lengthways or across, apples halved, quartered or sliced. Try to think of all the different marks that could be made – circles from sliced carrots, wedge shapes from quartered carrots or ovals from potatoes
2. Put out different coloured paint in saucers. Soaking sponges in paint does help to control the quantity of paint being used

PRINTING
1. Give a demonstration first – explain that it's not necessary to dip the printer into the paint every time (children tend to use far too much, but more interesting textured effects can be obtained if the printer isn't saturated). Emphasise they should 'print' not 'paint', which usually results in a muddy mess
2. Show how different shapes can be

overlapped and superimposed to make new shapes. Point out the changes in colour. A whole picture may be built up out of different shapes – houses, flowers, vehicles or simply a pattern. Encourage the children to fill up the paper
3 Older children may like to create a simple repeating pattern using one or two shapes
4 Encourage the use of different sides and edges of the vegetables. For instance the end of a stick of celery gives a good stippling effect, while lengthways produces lines
5 Try using the same colour paint to print on different coloured papers
6 Fill in larger shapes with prints to add interest to pictures – for example, brick shapes made with a piece of potato; or fill in the outline of an animal to make a textured skin – for example, a dinosaur

TO COMPLETE
The prints can be mounted as:
1 Pictures
2 Book covers
3 Wrapping paper
4 Greetings cards

HEDGEHOGS AND SQUIRRELS

MATERIALS
1. Thin card (suggested size 318mm × 254mm – one for each animal)
2. Scissors
3. Wax crayons in browns and black
4. Gummed paper – scraps of black and brown
5. Self-hardening clay or plasticine
6. Glue sticks

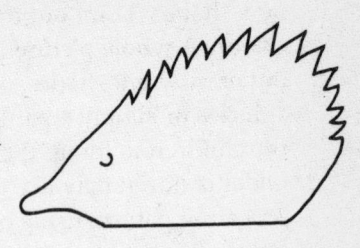

ADULT PREPARATION
1. Fold each piece of card in half lengthways
2. Copy the drawings opposite, so that the bases line up with the folds

MAKING UP
1. Cut out the animal shapes, taking care to cut through both thicknesses of card
2. Colour thickly with wax crayons, mixing colours
3. Scratch spiky lines on to wax of hedgehog's body using the points of scissors
4. Cut black eyes and brown nose out of gummed paper and stick on
5. Shape small rectangles of clay about 3cm × 2cm to make stands

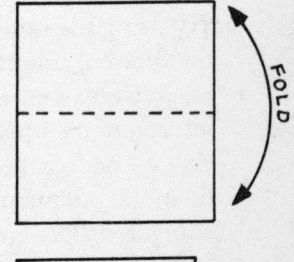

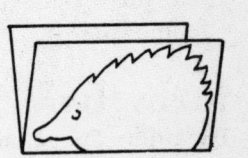

ASSEMBLING
1. Glue insides of the animals' faces to hold together
2. Press bases into mounds of clay

NOTE: Another way of making hedgehogs and squirrels is described on page 44.

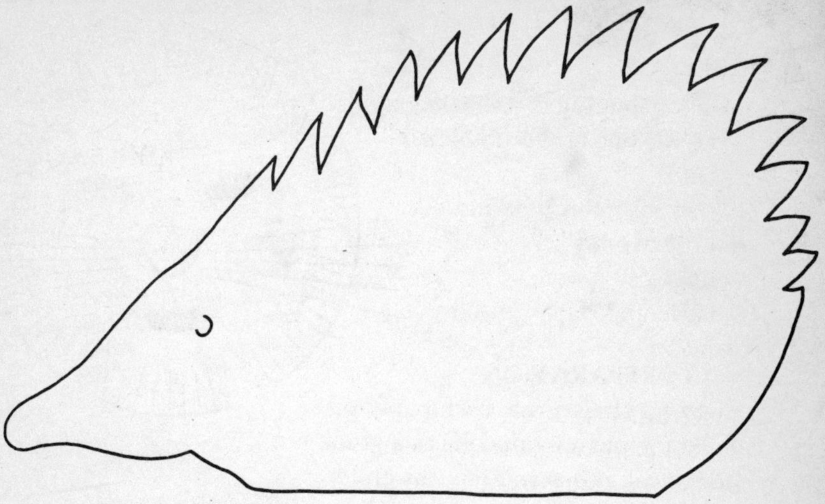

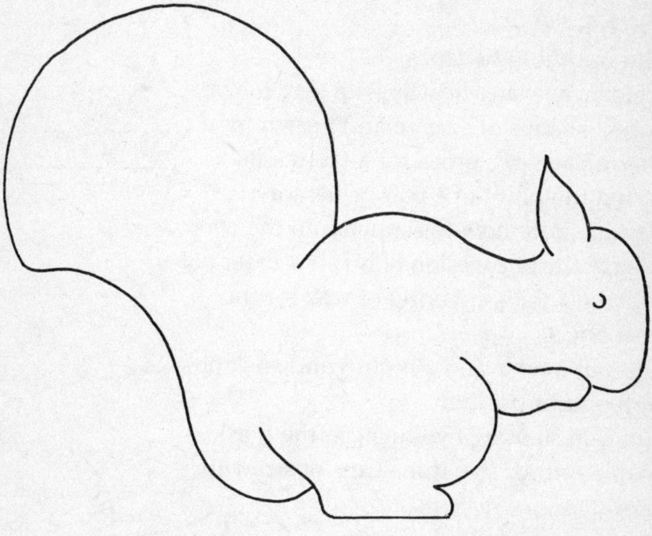

CAT MASKS

MATERIALS
1. White paper plates – one per child
2. Wax crayons in 'cat colours'
3. Scissors
4. Plastic drinking straws
5. Gummed paper
6. Stapler
7. Elastic

ADULT PREPARATION
1. Draw cat shape on to each paper plate using the picture opposite as a guide
2. Draw pink noses and mouths on to gummed paper
3. Cut straws into thin strips for whiskers

MAKING UP
1. Cut out the cat shapes
2. Colour the plates heavily with wax crayon – black, shades of orange and brown for a marmalade cat, greys for a tabby cat
3. Using the point of a pair of scissors, demonstrate how to scratch into the wax to give the impression of fur. It is essential to have a thick covering of wax for the best effect
4. Cut out a nose and a mouth and stick on in the right position
5. Cut two slanting eye-holes in the mask
6. Staple four or five thin strips of straw in position for whiskers
7. Staple elastic to each side to fit round the head – but not too tightly

LEAF SPATTER PICTURES

MATERIALS
1. A selection of leaves in a variety of shapes
2. Paper – either white or different pale colours
3. Old toothbrushes

ADULT PREPARATION
1. Simply cover surfaces with newspaper and put out the materials
2. This is messy, so ensure children are equally well covered!

MAKING UP
1. Arrange the leaves on a piece of plain paper
2. Secure the leaves with a small piece of Blu-Tack
3. Spatter by holding a toothbrush loaded with paint just above the picture and rubbing thumbs along the bristles. Several colours can be used
4. When the paper is sufficiently covered carefully remove the leaves to reveal leaf shapes in the colour of the paper

FURTHER IDEAS
1. Place other objects or shapes on the paper
2. Make a paper stencil to spray through
3. A less messy way to achieve a similar effect is to fill an empty non-aerosol household spray container (for window cleaner, for instance) with the paint. An old plant sprayer works well, too. Also see wax resist pictures on page 9

WALKING WITCH

MATERIALS
1 A sheet of thin card, about 26cm × 20cm
2 Compasses or a lid to draw round
3 Scissors
4 Pencils
5 Felt-tipped pens
6 Glue in a pot with a spreader
7 Glitter
8 Brass fasteners

ADULT PREPARATION
1 Copy the witch to the size needed
2 Figure 2 is a circle with crossing lines – these represent the witch's legs. Draw a circle and copy the legs so that they are of a size in proportion to your witch

MAKING UP
1 Cut out the witch and the circle
2 Colour the witch with felt tips, not forgetting the legs
3 Dab some patches of glue on to the witch's cloak and sprinkle with glitter
4 Make a hole through the centre of the circle with a brass fastener, moving it around a little so that it turns freely
5 Make a similar hole 2cm from the bottom of the witch
6 With the circle behind the witch line up the holes and join the two together with the brass fastener
7 If the witch is rolled gently along, the circle will rotate, making it look as if her legs are moving and she is walking!

40

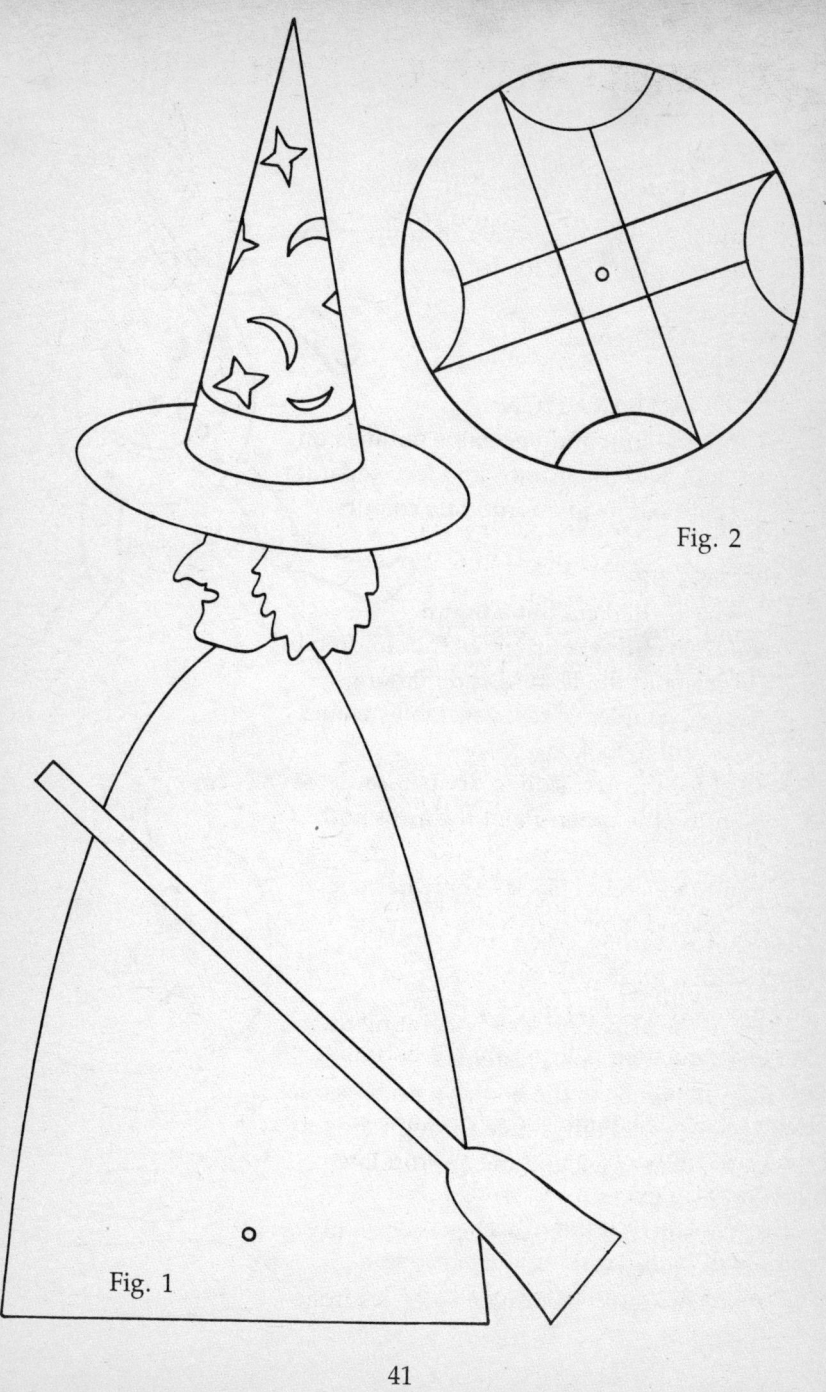

Fig. 2

Fig. 1

41

FRUIT AND VEGETABLE PEOPLE

MATERIALS
1. Thin white card
2. Paints – poster or powder in appropriate colours, plus black for faces
3. Scissors
4. Brass fasteners

ADULT PREPARATION
1. Copy the fruit and vegetable outlines on to card, with their arms and legs separate
2. Prepare paints in appropriate colours

MAKING UP
1. Let each child cut out a figure
2. Before painting, encourage the children to think about the texture and markings. Some examples of real vegetables would be useful to look at
3. Wait for the first side to dry before painting the other. Paint the arms and legs
4. Paint faces on in black – some help may be needed here

ASSEMBLING
1. Form the arms and legs by jointing them together with brass fasteners
2. Join the limbs to the bodies with brass fasteners, making a hole through the top of the arm or leg and the appropriate place on the body
3. Make sure the holes are big enough to allow movement
4. The figures can be hung as mobiles from the ceiling

43

GROUP ACTIVITY – AUTUMN TREE

MATERIALS
1. White blotting paper
2. Food colouring – red, orange, yellow, green
3. Waxed containers (such as margarine cartons) for mixing dye
4. Textured wallpaper (Anaglypta)
5. Wax crayons in shades of brown, grey, orange, green
6. A large sheet of paper in an autumnal shade (join two or three together, if necessary)
7. Scissors
8. Glue
9. Scraps of fur fabric
10. Drinking straws
11. Card for templates
12. Paper or thin card for creatures
13. Brown, green, and grey paint

ADULT PREPARATION
1. On the background paper draw a simple tree trunk shape
2. Make several leaf templates in card – oak, beech, etc
3. Mix up the dye by half filling waxed cartons with water and adding a few drops of food colour. Test for strength by dipping a small piece of blotting paper into the dye. If the colour is too weak, add some more drops
4. Make templates for the hedgehogs and squirrels, copying the drawings on page 37

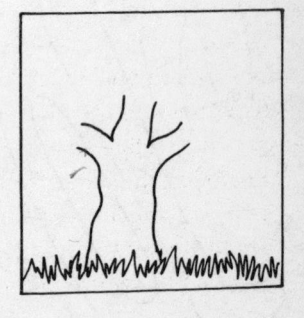

5 Cut out some bushy tails from fur fabric using the templates as a guide
6 Mix up the paint

MAKING UP
1 Let one group of children tear up small pieces of wallpaper and glue them to the background paper within the tree trunk lines
2 When all the gaps are filled in, colour the paper with shades of brown and grey wax crayon to create the impression of textured bark
3 Give the remaining children a sheet of blotting paper and the leaf templates. Draw round the templates and cut out the shapes. Four leaves per child should be sufficient
4 Add some patches of colour roughly with wax crayon, but don't cover all the white
5 One at a time, let the children dip their leaves in the dye. Make sure the dye is positioned well away from other activities. As the blotting paper absorbs the dye, rotate each leaf and very soon nearly all the white areas will be coloured. Dipping the leaves in more than one colour gives a more interesting effect where the colours merge

NOTE: You'll need to keep a close eye on the children at this stage.

6 Lay the finished leaves out on newspaper to dry

7 A couple of children could make grass at the base of the tree. To help them, simply draw a jagged line as a guide. The grass can either be sponge painted or made by sticking on pieces of green paper

To Make Hedgehogs
1 Draw round templates and cut out
2 For the spikes, cut drinking straws into 5cm lengths and stick them on to the body at a slant to resemble prickles
3 Paint the whole thing brown
4 Add the eyes and nose with a black felt pen

To Make Squirrels
1 Draw round templates and cut out
2 Glue on a tail
3 Paint the whole shape grey
4 Add features as above

ASSEMBLING
1 Glue dyed leaves to the tree – don't forget to have a few fluttering down as well as lying on the grass
2 Stick creatures into position under the tree
3 Captions describing autumn could be written on suitably coloured paper and positioned around the finished tree

🌿 CARDBOARD FIREWORKS

MATERIALS
1. Cardboard tubes – old loo rolls or kitchen paper rolls (cut shorter if necessary)
2. Paints and brushes
3. Glue stick
4. Fluorescent or shiny foil paper for streamers
5. Thin card in bright colours
6. Gummed paper in very bright colours
7. Scissors

ADULT PREPARATION
Make the rocket heads from brightly coloured thin card – or use white card and cover with gummed paper. Cut out circles of 10cm diameter and cut them in half – one semi-circle for each rocket

MAKING UP
1. Paint the cardboard tubes with bright-coloured patterns. Very young children may find it easier to paint with one colour and then apply sticky paper shapes when the paint is dry
2. Cut out strips of coloured paper to make streamers for the tail of the rocket. Then apply glue to the inside edge of the tube and stick on the streamers

TO COMPLETE
1. Form the semi-circle of card into a cone shape and staple it to the top of the tube
2. Mount the rockets on black paper with silver glitter stars scattered about

FOLDED PAPER SNOWMEN

Many other figures can be made in this way – clowns, scarecrows, soldiers, Santa Claus, even houses or Christmas trees. It makes a good decorative frieze.

MATERIALS
1. Strip of white paper approximately 12cm × 30cm
2. Scissors
3. Felt-tipped pens

ADULT PREPARATION
1. Measure 12cm from one end of the strip of paper and make a fold. Make another fold back, along the edge of the paper. Continue to concertina-fold the paper until the end of the strip
2. Keeping the paper folded, draw a picture of a snowman on the front

NOTE: Older children could probably manage both these for themselves, but ensure the snowman's arms go right off the edges.

MAKING UP
1. Cut out the snowmen, being very careful to leave their hands joining or the strip will fall apart (younger children will need a lot of help here)
2. Gently unfold the snowmen, who should all be holding hands!
3. With felt tips decorate the hats and draw in and colour scarves. Add black eyes, a red mouth and an orange nose. Each

snowman could be different – some happy, some sad

4 If liked, mount the snowmen on black or coloured foil paper. Join several together to form a long row or border

WINDOW CHRISTMAS CARD

This card can be made in two ways, both of which are described. For interest I have included two different scenes, though they are of course interchangeable – one looking in from outside, the other looking out from within. Perhaps you'll have further ideas of your own.

MATERIALS
1. Either sheets of white card, A4 size, or white card/acetate folders
2. Felt-tipped pens
3. Scraps of gummed and foil paper
4. Glue sticks
5. Scissors

Method I – interior scene, using folders made from white card with a clear acetate front (these are sometimes left over from business use)

ADULT PREPARATION
Out of white card, cut strips about 1.5cm wide and long enough to stick on to the acetate to create a window. For the edges of the frame, make the strips slightly wider

MAKING UP
1. Draw an interior Christmas scene inside on the white card – perhaps a tree surrounded by presents with decorations hanging from the ceiling. Use felt tips to colour
2. Stick on the white strips to make the window
3. Write on the back of the card

Method II – exterior scene, using white card where folders are not available

ADULT PREPARATION
1. Fold the white card in half and draw a simple window on the front
2. Cut out the four panes
3. On a piece of blue foil paper the same width as the folded card, draw an undulating line to indicate a landscape and cut it out. Do one for each card
4. Cut out a number of green foil paper triangles for simple fir trees

NOTE: Older children could do most of this for themselves.

MAKING UP
1. Glue the blue foil to the top of the inside of the card to form sky. The curving line should come about halfway down so that the uncovered white card forms snow-covered hills
2. Stick the fir trees into position
3. If you want to add something extra, use felt tips to draw a snowman against the white snow, with a brightly coloured scarf
4. Add gummed silver stars to the sky
5. If you make this scene using the acetate folder, cut some shapes out of gummed paper and stick them on the front, as if on a windowsill. I have included drawings of a cat, holly, and a bowl of fruit to give you some ideas

ANGEL MOBILE

MATERIALS
1 White card
2 Felt-tipped pens
3 Glue sticks
4 Glitter in different colours
5 Scissors
6 Christmas ribbons for hanging
7 Gold paint spray
8 Gold doilies

ADULT PREPARATION
1 Cut out an angel from the white card, copying the shape given
2 With a small dinner plate draw a circle on the white card. Use a smaller plate to make a second circle inside the first, leaving about 5cm between the two. Cut out the centre to form a ring
3 Copy the wing shape on to a gold doily (two for each angel)

MAKING UP
1 Colour the face pale pink, then add eyes and a mouth. Colour the hair yellow
2 Using a glue stick, lay a line of glue round the neck and bottom edge. Sprinkle on glitter. Spots of glitter can also be used on the angel's gown
3 Spray the ring gold, cover with foil, or dab with glue and sprinkle with glitter
4 Form the angel into a cone and staple it together at the back
5 Stick the doily wings wrong sides together and glue to the back of the angel
6 Make a small hole in the top of the head and thread a ribbon through. Hang the angel from the ring

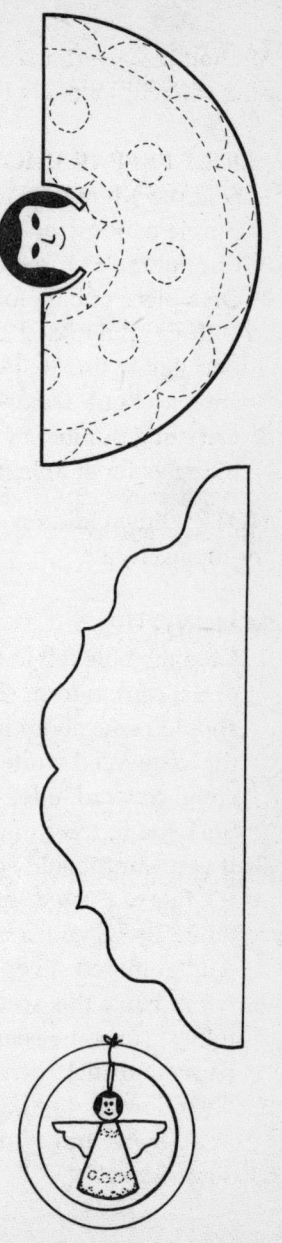

CLOWN FINGER PUPPETS

MATERIALS
1. Sheet of thin card (one per clown)
2. Pencils
3. Scissors
4. Felt-tipped pens

ADULT PREPARATION
Copy the clown directly on to the card (older children could try this for themselves)

MAKING UP
1. Cut out the clown. Be prepared to help with awkward bits like the ruffle
2. Colour in the clown. Encourage children to use bright colours – and to take time to decorate with patterns

TO COMPLETE
An adult *must* cut the two holes as indicated on the picture to fit the child's fingers, since this calls for sharp-pointed scissors

I have also included a snowman to give you at least one alternative idea to the clown – perhaps you'll think up some more yourself.

THE THREE BEARS

MATERIALS
1. Sheet of card – suggested size 20cm × 15cm
2. Pencil
3. Scissors
4. Crayons
5. Glue
6. Scraps of card for making finger holders

ADULT PREPARATION
Copy out the bears opposite on to the card

MAKING UP
1. Cut out the bears
2. Colour them in with crayons or felt tips
3. Older children might like to dress the bears with scraps of material and patterns are included opposite for this purpose

TO COMPLETE
1. Cut three strips of card 1cm wide and of a length to fit round the child's finger
2. Fold along dotted lines shown in Figure 1 and bend round to form a ring
3. Place a dab of glue at each end and stick to the back of one of the bears, roughly at the waist
4. When dry, the child can insert a finger into the ring and make the puppet move

Fig. 1

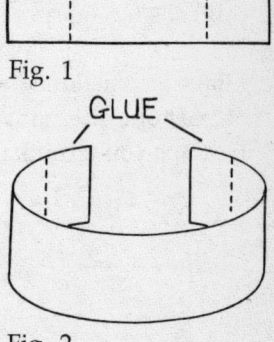

Fig. 2

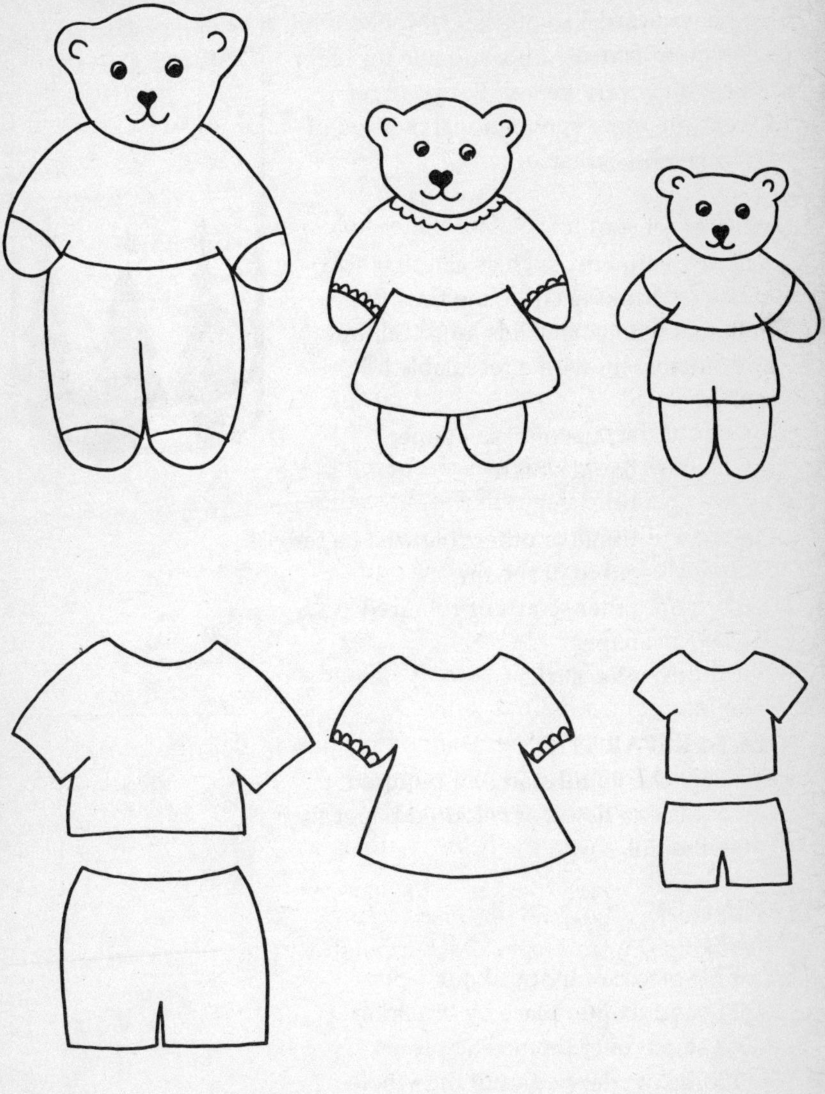

🌲 BISCUIT TINS

There are two methods for decorating tins. The first, using scraps of tissue applied with liquid starch, is really only suitable for older children – it is very messy! For younger children, the more conventional method of sticking is more suitable.

MATERIALS
1. Tall tins with lids, such as catering size coffee or drinking chocolate tins. Baby milk tins with plastic lids are ideal, but any suitable tin with a resealable lid will do
2. Either: a) scraps of tissue paper
   b) liquid starch
   c) brushes
   Or: a) tissue or other coloured paper cut to fit the tin
   b) other scraps of coloured paper
   c) glue sticks

ADULT PREPARATION
1. Make up the liquid starch, if required
2. Cut a piece of tissue or coloured paper to cover the tin

MAKING UP
Method I
1. Tear off pieces of tissue about 3–5cm square and fix into place by brushing liquid starch over them. The pieces should be overlapped until the whole tin is covered, applying starch over the top to keep the paper flat

2 When the coating has dried, a coat of clear varnish will give a nice finish and help to protect it

Method II
1 Glue the covering paper into position
2 Decorate the tins in a number of ways using gummed paper shapes or pictures cut from cards or magazines. Adapt the decoration to suit the season, using flowers and chicks for Easter, or red hearts for Valentine's Day
3 The illustration shows a tin decorated for Christmas. To do this, cut a strip of green crepe or tissue to fit round the tin and come about one-third up it. Fold it concertina fashion (see folded paper figures on page 48). Copy the Christmas tree shown below on to the folded paper and cut it out, leaving the ends of the bottom branches intact. Open out the frieze of trees and glue along the bottom edge of the tin. To complete the picture add a gold star to the top of each tree

TO COMPLETE
Fill the tins with biscuits – either bought or made from the recipe on the next page

🌳 BISCUITS TO FILL THE TINS

NOTE: An adult *must* deal with the hot oven.

MATERIALS
1. Biscuit dough from the recipe below
2. Cutters
3. Icing sugar and food colour
4. Hundreds & thousands, chocolate drops, angelica, glacé cherries etc
5. Small rolling pin
6. Flour
7. Greased baking trays

ADULT PREPARATION
Make up the biscuit dough as follows:
   225g (8oz) self-raising flour
   100g (4oz) margarine
   100g (4oz) sugar
   1 egg
   Rub the flat into the flour and stir in the sugar. Beat the egg and add it a little at a time, stirring, to form a stiff dough

MAKING UP
1. Let each child have their own rolling pin. Divide the dough into small balls
2. Roll out the dough balls to about 0.5cm thickness
3. With cutters appropriate to the occasion, cut out the biscuits. Use stars and fir trees for Christmas, cats for Hallowe'en, chick or egg shapes for Easter
4. If preferred, the dough could be moulded. For example, cut out a round for a face

and turn it into an Easter bunny by adding long ears shaped from the dough. After baking, decorate it with white icing, chocolate drop eyes and nose, with angelica whiskers

TO COMPLETE
1 Bake the biscuits for about 10 minutes in a fairly hot oven (Gas Mark 6, 200°C, 400°F). Allow to cool
2 Keep the biscuits in an airtight tin overnight if you want to decorate them the following day
3 Mix up the icing – children especially enjoy stirring in the colour, so supervision is important
4 Cover the biscuits with icing by drizzling a little at a time from a teaspoon

Here are a few ideas:
a) Black cats – colour the icing with cocoa and make eyes from angelica
b) Christmas trees – ice the biscuits with white or green and add silver balls or tiny sweets
c) Older children might like to make biscuit faces such as the Easter bunny described above or a clown. For this, ice the biscuit white; when that is dry, add some yellow icing for hair. Make eyes from black and white liquorice allsorts sliced across and a nose from a glacé cherry. Use two pieces of cherry placed side by side for red lips

🌳 WALLPAPER TREES

This picture can be adapted to suit a particular season

MATERIALS
1. Pieces of white textured wallpaper, about 30cm long
2. Wax crayons
3. Scissors
4. Large sheet of blue paper for the background
5. Green paint in a saucer and a small sponge
6. For the leaves (if required), scraps of tissue, gummed paper, paint or felt-tipped pens in appropriate colours
7. Glue stick

ADULT PREPARATION
Draw a simple tree trunk shape on to each piece of wallpaper

MAKING UP
1. Colour in the tree trunks using wax crayons (this brings up the texture of the paper). It's more interesting to use a mixture of colours: browns, greys, oranges, and greens, all blending
2. Cut out the trees – only older children will manage this on their own
3. Stick the trees on to a background paper – plan either to make a large group picture or a smaller individual one. In the first case, draw a line across a large sheet of blue paper and sponge-paint grass. For a

small picture, grass can be coloured in with crayons or felt tips
4 Glue trees into position

FINISHING
1 For winter, leave the branches bare and dab with white paint along the upper sides; replace green paint with white to make a snow scene. Dab more white paint or cotton wool in the sky for a finishing touch
2 There are several ways to make the leaves for summer and autumn:
   a) Sponge or brush paint on to the background paper using green for summer and russet colours for autumn
   b) Scrunch up small pieces of appropriately coloured tissue and stick on
   c) Tissue leaf shapes cut out and overlapped. This is especially good for autumn where a number of colours are used, but probably only suitable for older children who can handle scissors
   d) Gummed paper cut out and stuck on
3 For a spring picture, scrunched-up pink and white tissue makes very effective blossom and is a good contrast against painted leaves

GROUP ACTIVITY – PLAY DOUGH PICTURE

MATERIALS
1 Play dough made to the recipe below
2 Poster paints
3 Implements for making marks in the dough, such as pencils, blunt knives, nails, etc
4 Clear polyurethane varnish
5 Strong PVA glue
6 Hardboard for background
7 Biscuit cutters

RECIPE FOR PLAY DOUGH
2 cups of flour
1 cup of cornflour
1 cup of salt
Enough water to form a soft dough

NOTE: For this activity the dough is left white, but paint or food colouring can be added for other uses.

ADULT PREPARATION
1 Make play dough
2 Cut hardboard to required size and make two holes in the top for hanging. Thick, very stiff card could be used instead

MAKING UP
1 Give each child a lump of dough and a suggestion for a particular animal or figure
2 The dough can be roughly flattened with the hands, and heads, legs and arms squeezed and shaped. Add extra pieces of dough for hair or clothes

3 Mark features with a pencil or other pointed object

or

Roll out the dough and cut shapes out using a biscuit cutter or knife. Fir trees could be made this way using a Christmas tree cutter. Card templates are also useful to cut round

4 Leave the figures to dry for 24 hours, then paint and varnish them
5 Meanwhile paint the background using ordinary poster paint. (With several children, let them take turns at this)

TO COMPLETE
1 Arrange all the figures on the background and glue firmly in position
2 Attach some strong string to the top of the picture and hang it on the wall

SOME IDEAS FOR PICTURES
These instructions are for a large group picture, but individual ones can be made just as easily. Obviously pictures can show almost anything, but here are a few ideas to get you started:

Nativity scene – a simple stable can be created from sausage-shaped pieces of dough. A little gold glitter on white angel wings and stars in the sky would be a nice touch. Paint the Three Kings in rich colours and decorate their gifts with coloured glitter and their crowns with gold. To represent a night scene paint the background with a

dark-blue sky and dark-green hills
Street scene – include buses and cars, brightly painted houses (make tiled roofs from tiny balls of dough slightly flattened and pressed on), people, trees and flowers
Spring scene – with lots of animals, daffodils and tulips, and a big yellow sun in dough
Underwater scene – paint the background in blues and greens to look like water and make colourful exotic fish from the dough